PRAISE FOR RENEGADE PINKY

"It is the voice in these poems... y ironic. It is a voice I want to... r r

"How does the brain change suffering into art? As a neuroscientist, I can't say, but as a reader, I can report that it has happened. Andy Weatherwax, a polymath who has also produced musical and visual art, here brings his intense appreciation of the sensory world to the experience of illness. The result is transformative."

—Alice Flaherty, MD, PhD
Director, Movement Disorders, Mass. General Hospital
Author of *The Midnight Disease:
The Drive to Write, Writer's Block, and the Creative Brain*

"These poems reveal a depth of human spirit the reader will find to be a source of healing. Andy Weatherwax embraces his Parkinson's disease as a gift that allows him to love in new ways, to see with new vision, and to live with a sacred purpose. We see in his verse that he refuses to allow the Parkinson's to define him. Each poem bears witness to the quality of life one discovers when one moves beyond fear. Laced with the language of joy, this collection of Andy's work inspires us to live fully into each moment. Wisdom begins when we let ourselves be awed by the Creator. Andy is a wise human being."

—Rev. Richard C. Allen, Senior Minister
The Congregational Church in South Glastonbury, CT
United Church of Christ

"An honest, humorous, and at times, even lyrical, expression of the fragility and resilience of human life unfolding against the background of a greater compassion."

—Mark T. Unno, PhD
Shin Buddhist priest and scholar
Author of *Shingon Refractions:
Myoe and the Mantra of Light*

"The individual poems in Renegade Pinky are extraordinary. As a collection, the impact is breathtaking. These poems are informed by pain, uncertainty and loss; but even as we are brought to profound intimacy with these things, we as well accompany a poet possessing great good humor, an ironic take on life and exquisite sensitivity to the revelations of nature, music, love and everyday realities. Falling into a gutter, giving vent to anger, letting the words of Billie Holiday speak to him, turning the menace of a subway bully into kinship: such things mark Andy Weatherwax's days, and we emerge from our time with him aspiring to the deeper, broader, more creative and peace-filled ways of being human that infuse his life. I dare you to read these poems and not be changed."

—Alexandrina Sergio
Author of *My Daughter is a Drummer
in a Rock 'n Roll Band*

RENEGADE PINKY

RENEGADE PINKY

Poems and Prose

◆ ◆ ◆

ANDY WEATHERWAX

iUniverse, Inc.
Bloomington

Renegade Pinky
Poems and Prose

Copyright © 2012 by Andy Weatherwax.

All rights reserved. No part of this book may be used or reproduced by any means, graphic, electronic, or mechanical, including photocopying, recording, taping or by any information storage retrieval system without the written permission of the publisher except in the case of brief quotations embodied in critical articles and reviews.

iUniverse books may be ordered through booksellers or by contacting:

iUniverse
1663 Liberty Drive
Bloomington, IN 47403
www.iuniverse.com
1-800-Authors (1-800-288-4677)

Because of the dynamic nature of the Internet, any web addresses or links contained in this book may have changed since publication and may no longer be valid. The views expressed in this work are solely those of the author and do not necessarily reflect the views of the publisher, and the publisher hereby disclaims any responsibility for them.

Any people depicted in stock imagery provided by Thinkstock are models, and such images are being used for illustrative purposes only.
Certain stock imagery © Thinkstock.

ISBN: 978-1-4759-5116-5 (sc)
ISBN: 978-1-4759-5118-9 (hc)
ISBN: 978-1-4759-5117-2 (ebk)

Printed in the United States of America

iUniverse rev. date: 11/28/2012

This book is dedicated to Josefina and Tyler

◆ ◆ ◆

In Memoriam

Steve "Sinbad" Sinibaldi
and
Peter Saint Onge

CONTENTS

Foreword   xiii

PART 1: POSSESSION
- Lost and Found   3
- Possessive   4
- Renegade Pinky   6
- The Mask   8
- Thanksgiving Snow   9
- What Good Are These   11
- Old Man   12
- Mind, Body, and Me   13
- Indelible Reminders   14

PART 2: WAITING
- Waiting Now   19
- I Never Realized the Comfort a Gutter Could Offer   20
- Aground   22
- Does It Show?   23
- No Holiday   24
- Loneliness Sits   26
- Anticipating the Sun   27
- Another Night   28
- If I Dwell on It   32
- Raining Season   33
- This Day Go By   34
- And So It Goes   35

PART 3:	DOSE TO DOSE	
	Dose to Dose	39
	Rx Math	40
	Rx Math	41
	Insurance Coverage	42
	Procedures and Pills	43
	Authorization	44
	Medication Calculation	46
	Did Anyone Notice?	47
	The Nature of a Relationship	48
PART 4:	SPARK OPTIMISTIC	
	The Gift	53
	Three Weeks and Another Day	55
	There Are Days	56
	Most Beautifully	57
	Perfectly Blessed	58
	Illness Is My Teacher	60
	Released	62
	Brave, Fearful, Fool	63
	Never to Be Undone	64
	No Horseshoe Required	65
	Spark Optimistic	66
PART 5:	INDEED	
	Sorry Bunch	71
	Welcome to the NFL	74
	Indeed	76
	What Happened to Your Head?	79
	His Number	81
	Sunday Morning in the Village	83
	Pragmatics	84

PART 6: THORNS
    The Journey   89
    Fear Rides the Subway   90
    Vows   91
    Judgment   93
    To Be Free   95
    These Days, More Often Than Not . . .   98
    The Ocean Is My Teacher   100
    Easing into Traffic   102
    Only One Exception   104
    Almost Nirvana   106
    Misfortune and Heartache   107

PART 7: BLOSSOMS
    Sailing with Stravinsky   111
    Me and Walter and My '74 Hornet   112
    Miles Davis Knocks Buildings Over   114
    Red Sailing Cap   116
    For You, I Would Have Done Anything   117
    Crow   119
    Blossom   120
    This Thought   121
    Sometimes   122
    Title of This Poem   123

Afterword   125
Acknowledgments   129
About the Michael J. Fox Foundation   133
Cover Art and Chapter Illustrations   135
Chapter Quotations Bibliography   137

FOREWORD
Michael Burgan

A friend recently said I have a man-crush on Andy Weatherwax. I was taken aback at first, even a little defensive. Then I thought about it: Well, why not? If a guy's gotta have a man-crush, there are worse targets.

I tried to give the friend some context to understand how this crush came about. Andy and I have known each other since sixth grade. We spent countless hours together in a high school rock band. When most of our friends were away at college, we stayed, mostly, in our hometown and constantly hung out seeing movies, listening to music, talking. We spent nine weeks side by side backpacking through Europe. We have seen each other's best and worst moments and remained friends through it all.

But more telling than the *we* is the *he*: Andy has done amazing things. Or rather, he is amazing things—things I envy. A talented musician. A self-taught Internet marketing whiz respected in his field. A skilled woodworker. An accomplished sailor. A rock sculptor and self-published author of a book documenting that work. And, as this collection of poems you're holding shows, a writer with remarkably intelligent and honest insights into himself and poignant and wry observations of the world.

What's not to crush about?

Renegade Pinky demonstrates, over and over again, what I now most respect about Andy. He is a man courageously confronting Parkinson's disease. I've become more familiar with Parkinson's as Andy and his loved ones have tried to grapple with its effects. I have seen the physical deterioration, with the spasms and tightening muscles and fatigue. I've seen less of the emotional metamorphosis, the mood swings that are a combination of the drugs and the changes in the brain chemistry the illness brings. But I have seen the scar across his head, the reminder of the hidden implant now trying to restore some normalcy to his neurons, slowing down the ticking of the clock that means a few more cells are lost forever.

The battle with his nemesis Parkinson, as you can imagine, has not been easy, for him or his family and friends. But out of the struggle, Andy has found a deepening zest for life as he wrings out every experience and emotion he can, while he can. He has squandered nothing.

But, ultimately, *Renegade Pinky* is not about the man; it's about the words. It's like Frank Zappa says in "Blessed Relief." Wait a minute, he doesn't say anything in "Blessed Relief." It's an instrumental. But what he doesn't say in words, he says in music, and it's something I remember whenever I hear a beautiful tune, or absorb the power of a heartfelt poem, like so many in this book: Art helps make life worth living. Good art inspires us to seek deeper meaning of ourselves and the world around us. Life is too short to shut ourselves off from the beauty and passion that exist amidst the pain, the suffering, the chaos, the injustice. The diseases. Andy has learned that lesson. He lives it. He encourages us all to make that lesson—his lesson—our own.

That's enough. Anything I can say about the poet and his poems pales compared to experiencing them yourself. Go. Read. Enjoy. Understand. Live.

◆ ◆ ◆

Michael Burgan is an award-winning author of more than two hundred books for children and young adults, both fiction and nonfiction. His works include biographies of presidents, scientists, and explorers, and a graphic-novel adaptation of *Frankenstein* that was a Junior Library Guild selection. Also a playwright, Burgan's work has been produced across the United States. He currently writes on a variety of subjects at his blogs, *Crisis? What Crisis?* (http://mburgan.wordpress.com) and *The History Nerd* (http://thehistorynerd.wordpress.com). He lives in Santa Fe, New Mexico.

PART 1

POSSESSION

◆ ◆ ◆

Nobody would choose to have a disease visited upon them. Still, Parkinson's forced me to make a fundamental life decision: adopt a siege mentality, or embark upon a life journey.

—Michael J. Fox

◆ ◆ ◆

LOST AND FOUND

I have Parkinson's disease
I thought you should know
in case you see him
please tell him so

I hope he's not worried,
dismayed, or concerned,
he's not the only one
who'd like to see it returned

POSSESSIVE

There are few words more ambiguous in meaning than *possession*.
The dictionary says possession is the act of having
      or taking into control.
In legal terms it can mean occupancy of property,
      without regard for ownership,
or without regard for legality, as with drugs or weapons.

Possession can also refer to control of a ball or puck;
or domination by something—a spirit, a passion, an idea;
or a psychological state in which
      an individual's normal personality
is replaced by another.

But possession is most often associated with ownership,
though it need not refer to literal ownership.
Sure, we can speak of Bob's hat if Bob owns a hat,
but we can also speak of Bob's children
      even if Bob doesn't own them.

Which brings me to Parkinson's disease.

It's a funny name for it.
I have it, yet it is not mine.
Parkinson never had it; he just found it.
Now I have it; now it's my Parkinson's disease.

We would never speak of my Bob's hat,
just makes no sense.
Anyhow, that's not the point.
The point is it's possessive.

That is exactly what it is.

RENEGADE PINKY

a renegade pinky and a heavy left foot
I can no longer type and my mambo's kaput
see, there's part of my brain that's neurotransmitter low
the part that helps me move, helps me get up and go

now my head can't tell my limbs what to do
it's been overthrown in a gray-matter coup
my mind's on fire, and my body won't move
so I may look stiff, but I've still got my groove

my renegade pinky runs happy and free
deciding on its own when to press down a key
making it tough to type this melodic phrase
taking time to delete extra s's and a's

and I'm no Fred Astaire when I'm cutting the rug
I've got my own boogie I call the "brain bug"
my samba might swing like a toilet seat
but you can't touch my tango for two left feet

I don't pen these words for sympathy
just thought you should know what's gotten into me
I may be ill, but I solemnly vow
to live out my days in the here and now

so I hope you understand that as of today
I've got a new approach to extra *s*'s and *a*'s
it is what it is, I write to decree
from here on out, fuck the baaack ssspaaace key

THE MASK

it's not the stiffness in my legs every morning when I wake
it's not the slowness with which I move or the lumber of my gait
it's not the hesitation every time I reach a door
in crowds or just around the house as I shuffle across the floor

it's not the pain that courses through my back and hips and feet
it's not the twinge with every bend or graceless way I eat
it's not the way I fumble with my wallet at the store
as the cashier wonders why for me counting change is such a chore

it's not that gourmet's now a bore with muted sense of smell
it's not the way I toss and turn in search of comfort for a spell
it's not the fact that all of these make difficult my day
nor that bedtime nightmares give me pause to hit the hay

it's none of these nor many more that causes me most pain
it's the mask I wear that hides me from my love that is my bane

THANKSGIVING SNOW

bright and quiet, a blanket of white
over autumn's final leaves
the tree's stark limbs, covered
hung heavy, slouching, burdened

there was music in my heart
as we rolled a base until it was too big to move
then a torso, and a head

Tyler giggled and bounced about
yelling, *no man! no man!*
not yet able to get around the *s*

Josa got a carrot for his nose and a Red Sox cap for his head
I got sticks for his arms and stones from the driveway
     for his mouth and eyes
he was a sight to behold, arms akimbo and vacant grin

home movies documented the day
Tyler's eyes wide with excitement, his smile honest and open
Josa's spirited laugh inspired and enthusiastic

there was music in my heart, a beautiful melody stirred
but it could not be heard by anyone but me
there was a disconnect

my blank face, uncoupled
hung heavy, slouching, burdened
the outside world could not see my smile
that day it snowed on Thanksgiving

WHAT GOOD ARE THESE

what good are these legs
if they can't take me to you

and these hands
if I can't pen the words you're reading

and these arms
if I can't wrap them round and round you

pull you close and say
welcome to another perfect day

OLD MAN

I'm feeling old, man
like the one-hundred-year-old man

losing patience with old-man self
I shuffle here and stumble there
I fumble with this and grumble at that
and mumble to my old-man self

I'm feeling old, man
like the one-hundred-year-old man
feeling every bit of
one hundred years old
man

MIND, BODY, AND ME

once I was one
now I am three
mind, body, and me

as each day passes
I feel my body slipping
and my mind straining
to stay sound in the face of betrayal

as each day passes, the burden weighs heavier
dragging mind, body, and me
step after step

as each day passes, the burden weighs heavier on her
as she drags mind, body, and me
day after day

once I was one
now I am three
mind, body, and me

INDELIBLE REMINDERS

the tremor in my arm
    and the pain in my back
        are indelible reminders
            of the cells I lack

my brain was fine until
    a gray-matter attack
        sent my dopamine levels
            to the red from the black

PART 2

WAITING

◆ ◆ ◆

Health is the greatest gift, contentment the greatest wealth, faithfulness the best relationship.

—Buddha

◆ ◆ ◆

WAITING NOW

a mourning dove's hollow cry
the first colors of spring from forsythias
a long since dead tree, branchless, points to a new blue sky

I am waiting now, gazing out the window
it's quiet and no one is home

I am waiting now, pecking at these keys
one finger, one letter at a time
laboring, slow to get these   words   down

I am waiting now, shuffling across the floor
writhing in my seat, slouching over the keys, tapping another line
shuffle, writhe, slouch, tap—and time lingers

the promising warble of a song sparrow, confident and optimistic
my left foot dances as my wait grinds toward that first sign of relief
the grip loosens
the door opens
they are home

I type this line with ease

I think I'll have a cup of tea

I NEVER REALIZED THE COMFORT A GUTTER COULD OFFER

a rattle in my head, fatigue in my bones
into a gutter on the corner of 96th and 3rd I fall

feeling oddly quiet, I lie peaceful and calm
a little rest had been in order

with the perspective of an ant
I watch the shoes and socks
of all walks step over me

and I listen to the crunch and grind
where feet meet the street

I lie and wonder
shall I pick myself up?
or is this the time I stay down, never to rise?

no dreams to lift me, no imagination to carry me
nothing to comfort me, just an empty sleep
odorless,
colorless,
humorless,
sleep

rolling over I see the sky above
I feel a pebble on my cheek

best get up before I fall too deep

AGROUND

I ran aground again
grinding to a halt
no chance for drift
so here I'll sit
unable to buoy
confident the tide will return
as it does every day
to lift me from these sardonic sands

DOES IT SHOW?

delight
and down
best get out of town
before she meets my
distant gray frown

he comes
and goes
but no one knows
why hide from them
'cause I fear it shows

NO HOLIDAY

dripping with sweat in the oppressive city heat
typical this time of year
back throbbing, knotted feet
keep me tethered to my seat

struggling to keep tears at bay
I sit across from my destination
putting final touches on a four-hour presentation
for those eager to hear what I have to say

sipping my coffee, I wait
for immobility to abate
and I listen as the haunted melancholy of Billie Holiday
fills the bustling coffeehouse . . .

he ain't got rhythm
so no one's with him
the loneliest man in town

true that, Billie
as if for me she sings
a counterpoint to the morning rush

I can only watch as they gracefully juggle coffee, papers, and purses
they walk, they talk, they smile
some gawk at me trying to move

I've lost my groove
ill at ease and fatigued to the bone
with anguish and determination
Lady Day pours her aching sorrow into the room . . .

I'm so weary and all alone
feel tired like heavy stone
who will see and who will care
'bout this load that I must bear
trav'lin', trav'lin' all alone

true that, Billie
as if with me she flirts

her phrasing, her voice
can't help but listen
who cares what I have to say

this ain't no holiday
another business trip
another day

LONELINESS SITS

loneliness sits at this desk
with the door closed
hoping no one knocks for five more minutes

loneliness stands at the counter
and apologizes for the mess
grateful for another cup of coffee

loneliness shuffles through crowds
and arrives at the platform
in time to watch as the train departs

loneliness takes the final turn home
to a house on a hill
and is greeted with open arms by a loving family

loneliness sits at this keyboard
and pecks at these keys
trying to string together the words
any words
to say something
anything
that will ease the burden

loneliness sits in silence at 4 a.m.
and wonders what 5 a.m. will bring

ANTICIPATING THE SUN

me and the foghorn,
the seagull, the cricket,
and the distant rattle of a delivery truck

anticipating the sun
me and the hermit crab, this keypad, the day's first light
and the optimism that is 4 a.m.
another opportunity
to get
this
day
right

anticipating the sun
me and all the others
eager to put another sleepless night to bed

what's next, when all's said and done?
me and another broken moment
anticipating the sun

ANOTHER NIGHT

It happened again. Nightmares. I woke screaming twice. I'm sitting in front of the TV. It is 3 a.m.

Flip.
Late-night talk shows I did not know exist.

Who are these people?
How do they lure their guests?
Who are their guests?

Flip.
A young, well-dressed, and overly enthusiastic man is gently kneading something called a "luxury gel fiber bed" that he really wants me to have. He is wired and says that the bed is "the next-best thing to a ride in his private jet to sleep on clouds."

I'm thinking he might be on drugs.

Moving to the blankets, he picks one up and tosses it on the floor. He gets on top of it and writhes about, then rolls himself up in it, telling me that "There's nothing better than wrapping yourself up like a little burrito."

Yeah, he's on drugs.

Flip.
"The Magic Bullet is the personal versatile countertop magician that *does any job in ten seconds or less*! With *no cleanup*!" It grinds and chops, it's a personal fruit-smoothie maker, it has a specially designed shaker top, it's the ultimate party machine, it's got multicolored comfort rings, it's an ingenious extractor, it's, it's, it's . . .

Come on! It's a miniature blender! And that's a miniature onion!

Flip.
"You're going to love my nuts!"

What the . . . !

Flip.
Two women with a combined eight inches of cleavage are telling me I don't have to do anything; the website sells the "Greatest Vitamin in the World" for me. Cleavage One asks the questions, like, "You mean to tell me if I get *just ten people* to try, *I get a check for* $1,000?" and Cleavage Two answers with stuff like, *"Exactly!" "Absolutely!"* and *"That's right!* This is the easiest way in the world to start *generating* $1,000 *checks over and over again!"*

Mmm, cleavage. I'm sorry, you were saying?

Flip. Flip. Flip.
Robert Tilton is talking to me. "Hallelujah!" he shouts. "If you really love Jesus, make a $1,000 vow of faith *now*! Then you will know the true blessings of the Lord and get out of the financial hole you're in!"

I'm not sure I understand, Bob. How could parting with 1k help ease financial burden?

"Oh, I know you probably don't have $1,000 . . ."

This is what I am saying, Bob!

He continues with some specifics now: "There are fifteen of you out there!" he shouts, hands held high. "At least fifteen who need to make a $1,000 vow! *Now*!"

Yeah, $1,000, I got it! Bob, have you met the Cleavage Twins?

He pauses, looks directly into the camera, and smiles like the cat that got the cream. "Praise the Lord! *He* has great things in store for those who *walk in faith*!"

I watch as he works himself into a frenzy. He shuts his eyes tight and begins to tremble. His face twitches and reddens. He shakes his clenched fists at me and lets out an indecipherable howl: *"Al so ro bahka!"*

The veins on his neck swell. His twisted face glistens with sweat. He is shaking as if possessed—as if his head is going to pop off! He is screaming now. *"Foul, rotten, stinkin' devil! I'm going to beat you up, you devil! I'm going to cut you to pieces in the name of Jesus!"*

Jeez, Bob, maybe lay off the coffee! You're starting to scare me.

He calms down and opens his eyes again. There is a bit of white foam in the corner of his mouth. Catching his breath, he wipes his brow, looks at me, and calmly says,

"There is someone watching right now, right *now*, who can't sleep! You need to make a vow of faith!"

What are the odds?
Where's that checkbook?
Amen.

IF I DWELL ON IT

immobility, like setting concrete
wraps me like a dead Egyptian king
in the desert heat, where anxiety looms

if I give an inch, it takes me
mile after mile
down a barren road

to a house with no windows
and a dog in the yard, barking

barking at nothing

nothing at all

RAINING SEASON

I
drop
emotion
at the drop
of a hat, in the
raining season my
desert face thirsts
now drinking in
every tear

THIS DAY GO BY

through a blurred lens I peer at a life out of focus
straining to recognize the faint outlines of vague impressions
in obscured appreciation of this point in time

my isolation doesn't want to be around anyone
my condition doesn't want to walk or talk or think
no need to say or do anything

in a haze
through narrowed eyes
I watch this day go by

AND SO IT GOES

the lull sucks
taut, awkward
anxious to sit
bound and on edge

"leave me alone!"

nosing up
writhing, fidgeting
ready to move
loosened from the hold

"hey, where are you going?"

temporary salvation
fast fading

and so it goes

day in, day out
up and down

and so it goes

PART 3

DOSE TO DOSE

◆ ◆ ◆

He who is not courageous enough to take risks will accomplish nothing in life.

—Muhammad Ali

◆ ◆ ◆

DOSE TO DOSE

meetings and meals are just a couple of ways
that some people go about segmenting their days
the carefree student moves from class to class
the beer-drinking bum drinks from glass to glass

I, on the other hand, have my own special way
of going about dividing my day
it all began when I was first diagnosed
now it's days of drugs from dose to dose

RX MATH

let's see if I have this right
I take
5 at 6
2 at 8
2 at 10
3 at 12
2 at 2
2 at 4
2 at 6
4 at 9
and sometimes 2 at 11
that makes 22
sometimes 24
I'm pretty good with numbers
always have been

RX MATH

(Showing the Work)

let's see if I have this right
I take
~~1 2 3 4~~ 5 at 6
2 at 8
+ 2 at 10
~~1 2 3 at 9~~
~~1 2 3 4 5~~ 3 at 12
~~1 at 2~~ 2 at 2
~~1 2 3 at 3~~
2 at 4
~~and~~
~~1 2 3 at 6~~ 2 at 6
~~and sometimes~~
~~1 2 at 9~~
4 at 9
and sometimes 2 at 11
that makes ~~4 6 10 12 18~~ 22
sometimes ~~11 13 19~~ 24
I'm pretty good with numbers
always have been

INSURANCE COVERAGE

March is up and I'm 6k down
    give me more shit and I'll paint the town

as each year wanes I'm covered less
    but my body needs more as I regress

PROCEDURES AND PILLS

procedures and pills are needed to solve
my left side's independent resolve
the effects on the side of condition and pill
got me to the doc for another drill

an hour I wait; in a minute she found
the need for blood, drug, and an ultrasound
that's bullshit, doc, I know what I need
and it's not another scan or poison seed

the *industry* of health I dare malign
snake-oil sales to boost the bottom line
greed will pave the way from birth to knell
if you leave it to them and the shit they sell

call me a cynic, but the lesson's learned
your well-being is not a top concern
no time to talk, to see forest through trees
they often overlook the overarching disease

AUTHORIZATION

The woman on the other end of the phone asked me if I really need it. That's what she said: "Do you really need it?" This, to me, was cause for concern.

I was not sure how to respond to her question.

Perhaps she was a neurologist—one with a firm understanding of movement disorders. One so familiar with my situation as to have thoughts of her own as to the best way to manage my illness. She didn't sound like a neurologist. And, besides, what neurologist worth a damn would be answering calls for an insurance company?

You see, my doctor, a real neurologist, suggested that I add a new medication to my Rx cocktail—one that will help me with the deep fatigue brought about by my condition and the narcolepsy-like sleepiness that is a side effect of another drug in my cocktail, a drug which also keeps me up some nights with vivid hallucinations.

And I needed authorization from the insurance company. I am not sure why they care. I mean, I get $800 per year coverage. I ingest $1,827.24 worth a month. This does not include the cost of nutritional supplements clinically proven to help slow the progression and ease the symptoms. Regardless, supplements are not deemed worthy of coverage, so this point is moot.

So, do I really need it?

I paused a moment, then told her that in fact I do not really need it; I just wanted to see if I could break $2k per month for drugs.

No response.

I then told her that, in all seriousness, it's for my lazy cat.
Again—nothing.

I began snoring.

"Sir, are you all right?"

Okay, I made that last one up. But, really, what's up her ass? I'm the one who needs the damn drug!

MEDICATION CALCULATION

Today is the last day in a month of days that has had me on the run nonstop. It culminates at 8:45 p.m. this evening. I'm presenting to a group of five hundred or so in New York City.

I usually take my first dose at 6 a.m. to kick the day in the ass. But I don't think that will work today.

By my calculation I need to move things up an hour; 7 a.m. and I should be good.

Let's see, 7 a.m., 10 a.m., 1 p.m., 4 p.m., 7 p.m. By the time I'm done, it will be 9:45 p.m., fifteen minutes until I start to fade.

DID ANYONE NOTICE?

I'm about halfway through my presentation when I look at the time and notice that five minutes have passed since I was to have taken my next dose. That makes me nervous.

And I feel my body beginning to slow.

I reach into my pocket and jingle my meds like loose change.

A man in the back raises his hand.

"Yes," I say, pointing in his direction.

Heads turn as he poses his question.

I stroll back to the podium, pull the pills from my pocket, and in one motion I pop them into my mouth.

I take a swig of water.

"Great question," I say.

I don't think anyone noticed.

I'm good to go.

THE NATURE OF A RELATIONSHIP

my wife keeps me strong
my son keeps me motivated
my family keeps me confident
my friends keep me true
you all keep me going
for this I am grateful

but I would be remiss not to acknowledge
my new friends, *meds*

oh, our relationship has had its ups and downs
they piss me off at times, the self-righteous bastards
and I've resented them
for breaking up my day
for making me wait
for getting stuck in my throat
for reminding me that I forgot
for making me sleepy during the day
for keeping me up at night
for the nightmares and nausea
for draining my bank account
for the authorizations and paperwork
for being necessary

despite all this, I am grateful
I'm not sure what I would do without them

besides, we have little choice in the matter
it is an arranged marriage

so I'm adjusting my attitude about my new friends
we can make this work
I'll try to be more accepting and understanding
if they will

that is, after all,
the nature of a relationship

PART 4

SPARK OPTIMISTIC

♦ ♦ ♦

I can't change the direction of the wind, but I can adjust my sails to always reach my destination.

—Jimmy Dean

♦ ♦ ♦

THE GIFT

this is a gift
and I am ill with it

it bounces around my brain
slowly seizing my ability
to move
to speak
to think

this is a gift, I told my six-year-old son
not the type you wrap with a bow
not a gift you would wish upon anyone

there was a time when my musings strayed to madness
my thoughts to terror

there was a time I would blame the moon
for its blurred reflection in turbulent waters

but gratitude's exquisite blossom now fills my heart
leaving fear no recourse

clarity returns, and I can see the moon

this is a gift of understanding of the suffering
caused by illness, old age, and death

this is a gift of compassion
that puts self-pity in the past
the future is forever now

I breathe
the clear sky above my head
the vegetable garden at my feet

this is a gift
and I am alive with it

THREE WEEKS AND ANOTHER DAY

three weeks and a day have passed
the fog is lifting
wounds are healing
as the day's last pain
courses through my body

three weeks and a day have passed
life is beckoning
the rhythm of time returns
and the day's last song
eases the burden

three weeks and a day have passed
and I am awake
ready to get on with it
as the day's last thought
turns to gratitude
in anticipation of
three weeks and another day

THERE ARE DAYS

there are days I walk all day living
on these days I am at peace

dwelling in the moment
embracing my life

seeing every flower
hearing every bird
and the rain bouncing off leaves
tires on the wet road
a barking dog in the distance

there are days I walk all day living
and there are days that I do not

there are days I walk all day living
and today is one of those days

MOST BEAUTIFULLY

harassed by thoughts
thought conquered long ago

searching for answers to questions never asked
wanting solutions to problems that do not exist

longing for what has been
yearning for what has yet to be

expectations lead to waiting
while each moment is lost to the past

today is perfect

remembering this
allows me to live
most beautifully

PERFECTLY BLESSED

I'm tired of dressing myself in the morning
    I'm tired of getting tangled in shirts
    struggling with buttons and shoelaces
    wrestling with socks and pants
    I'm tired of frustration with the simplest of tasks

I'm tired of the sound of my feet shuffling along the floor
    I'm tired of the clumsiness
    tripping over toys
    running into tables and walls
    I'm tired of the bumps and bruises

I'm tired of Medusa's stare
    the tension in my body
    the rigidity in my limbs
    and the cramps in my feet
    I'm tired of pulled muscles and pinched nerves

I'm tired of tasteless food in an odorless world
    being a prisoner to medication
    sitting at my desk waiting to move
    sitting in my car waiting to move
    I'm tired of feeling like dead weight

I'm tired of the ups and downs
    the tears
    feeling strange
    and feeling like a stranger

I'm tired of rush-hour traffic, rude people, marketing and advertising, politics and politicians, fevered egos and self-indulgence

I am tired of the evening news

I am tired of the suffering
and I am tired of being tired

I am mindful of my tired self
    mindful of the roof over my head
    the bird at the window
    the bed beneath me

I am mindful of this moment

smiling at my pillow
I am grateful for a place to lie and rest
I close my eyes
perfectly tired
and perfectly blessed

ILLNESS IS MY TEACHER

I'd like to run with the boys,
cook dinner on an open flame,
and enjoy a glass of wine
with friends and family

grasping at the past, I weep
an icy wall of anger and resentment
frozen, unable to break free from this frigid barrier
that holds hardened self-pity near and dear

I close my eyes and listen
to the sounds of the summer barbecue,
the laughter of the boys,
the chatter of friends and family

I close my eyes and breathe
letting the warm waters of gratitude
thaw the raw grip of expectation,
letting go of *I wish,* letting reality, as it is, arise

I close my eyes and smile
it is what it is
and there's no way to escape it

I am of the nature to grow old, to fall ill, to die
everyone whom I love and all that I hold dear
is of this same nature
this I learn time and again
humbled by illness, my great teacher

RELEASED

staring at the sun as it flattens through naked limbs
I hear the trickle of a distant brook waiting for the moon
as the day's last shadow slithers to tomorrow

a crow is laughing at me from the twisted limb
of an empty cottonwood tree

these days, sitting on the porch
listening to the slowing rhythm of a lone cricket
I am released by life's bittersweet song

BRAVE, FEARFUL, FOOL

some say I handle it well
some say I am brave
they say, *You're so brave*

a thread is all that keeps fear from the brave
a fine line is all that separates the brave from the foolish

sensei says,
The fool who knows he's a fool
is a wise man
the fool who thinks he is wise
is a fool indeed

sometimes I am brave
sometimes I am fearful
often I am a fool

remembering this allows me to crack wise
at my continued and slow demise

NEVER TO BE UNDONE

pulling myself from this hole
dusting off with heart and soul
your love picked me up
now I'm pouring it back into your empty cup

shredding all the past mistakes
my heart stirs each breath you take
giving up to bliss
is something I really wouldn't wanna miss

rather than reminisce
come in close for the final kiss
what's the point of this
what good is love without a heart at risk

    never to be undone
    there are no guarantees
    I pull myself from this hole
    I'm gonna get on up now
    and set my passion
    free

NO HORSESHOE REQUIRED

I walk under ladders, don't knock on wood
I'm stupidly happy; my life is quite good

with each tick of time, I stride with more spring
no matter the way luck's pendulum swings

you can't douse my spark; my cup remains full
each joker I'm dealt fans my flames higher still

I don't stake my claim on cards I have not
there is no choice but to play what I've got

I may be ill, but I'm happy and free
'cause I'm not my illness and it is not me

so I walk under ladders, things goin' my way
no horseshoe required, not even today

SPARK OPTIMISTIC

it is 5 a.m.
and the muted glow of morning
reveals the day's first shadow
and sparks the optimistic cacophony
of sparrow's song
chickadee's whistle
robin's whinny
cardinal's call
crow's caw
catbird's chatter
and others marking the first bars of another day

it is 5 a.m.
and brilliant new leaves gently twist about
eager to pop from dull red buds

it is 5 a.m.
and asparagus pokes its head through the damp earth
to see the first leaves of strawberries and chives

it is 5 a.m.
a doe gazes at me as I pull open the door
and step into the mild breeze
I think to myself, *nature is very cool*

it is 5 a.m.
I take a sip of coffee and wait
for my muted glow
to spark optimistic

PART 5

INDEED

◆ ◆ ◆

Do not spoil what you have by desiring what you have not; remember what you now have was once among the things you only hoped for.

—Epicurus

◆ ◆ ◆

SORRY BUNCH

An overweight businessman chews his tongue like cud
peering down his nose at the goings on around him.
We make eye contact. *how are you today?* I ask.
He stops chewing just long enough to grunt and nod.

And momma's boy and his momma sit across from me.
He didn't sit right, he didn't stow the bags right,
he didn't hand her the paper right,
I think he's too old to get so much so wrong.

I am unable to move, waiting, as I often do,
for medication to release me; comfort is fleeting.

A young mother with a baby carriage struggles onto the train.
Momma's boy and cud chewer have placed their bags in the aisle
and the carriage will not fit.
And they will not budge.

I struggle to my feet and lend a hand
lifting the carriage over the bags.
I am the object of momma's snarl and cud chewer's grunt.
Young mother says *thanks* with a smile.

A tense-looking woman offers her seat to mother and child.
Passing me and cud chewer and momma's boy
she mutters under her breath, *some gentlemen.*
Can't say I disagree.

Tense woman is now standing
and a man boards, he is on crutches.
Tense woman stares and continues her muttering
as crutches struggles to get by the same obstacles.

I speak up. *why don't you guys put your bags in the rack?*
Cud chewer pulls his bag onto the seat next to him.
Momma's boy looks for a cue from momma.
Tense looks me in the eye, shakes her head in apparent disgust.

I smile, she frowns.
How am I part of the problem?
My drugs kick in, and the train pulls out.
I can move, albeit spastically.

I'm compelled to see what tense is all about.
I stand and approach. *That was very kind of you to give up your seat.*
Someone had to, she snipes, *Common courtesy.*
Certainly, I say, *you are welcome to my seat.*

The train rounds a bend,
I trip and stumble toward her, nearly wiping out.
She flinches, recoils and brings her arms to her chest
and looks at me as if I wanted to grope her or something.

I grab the back of cud chewer's seat and regain my composure.
Cud chewer looks back at me and grunts.
Tense looks at me like I am drunk.
I can't win.

I decide to lay my version of guilt down for tense:
Sorry, I have a touch of Parkinson's disease.
I feel like an idiot.
What a sorry bunch.

WELCOME TO THE NFL

It was late and I was tired.
The cramp in my foot and the pain in my back were agonizing.
Gripping the handrail, I took one last look around.
Clear of hurried commuters, I lumbered down the long stairway.

With each step I got that much closer to the platform,
that much closer to home.
With just a few steps to go, I hear him:
"Jesus Christ, could you move any slower!"

I turned to face a tall, distinguished-looking businessman
barking these angry words.
He wore a gray suit, carried a leather briefcase.
I was the object of his rage.

Everyone on the crowded platform fell silent.
"Sorry," I said, "I have Parkinson's disease, and . . ."
"I have prostate cancer!" he bellowed. "Welcome to the NFL!"

I have prostate cancer? Welcome to the NFL?

The thought occurred to me
this was perhaps the first time this phrase had ever been uttered.

We had the platform's undivided attention
as this impromptu bit of performance art unfolded.
Smiling, I placed a hand on his shoulder. "I'm sorry."
I felt for the guy, angry—and perhaps drunk—as he was.

But we were not on the same page.
He would have nothing of it.
"Thank you very much for making me miss my train!
You are an evil, very evil man!"

Well now, this is awkward.

The silent platform looked on, eagerly awaiting the conclusion:
prostate cancer versus Parkinson's disease.
It's Parkinson's move . . .

a.) "I'll see your cancer and raise you an irritable bowel!"

b.) "Thank you! Thank you! And for my next heinous act of evil, I will fumble with change at the ticket counter!"

c.) "The secret of health for both mind and body is to live in the present moment, wisely and earnestly."

d.) Smiling, I turned away.

How is one to respond?

INDEED

He must have been 6'5" with broad shoulders and a menacing grin.
His jet-black skin glistened with sweat in the bright sunlight
on this sticky summer day.
Leaning on an umbrella, he flirted with two women.

Such was the scene directly in front of the entrance to the men's room
I so desperately needed to visit.
Anyone having to take a leak
would have to run this gauntlet.

He saw me shuffling toward them.
Our eyes met, he paused midsentence and grinned.
After a moment he continued his chatter,
all the while keeping his gaze on me
and grinning that menacing grin.

My unhurried advance became comical,
step after step, so slow to reach my destination.
When I was close enough to engage, he did.
"Looks like you're having a good ol' time, bro!"

I don't bother to try to understand comments like that.
Some people think I'm drunk.
If they think me a drunk, then I am a drunk.

"It's a beautiful day, my man!" I replied.
I said hello to the two ladies and shuffled into the men's room.

He was waiting for me when I finally exited.
Through a hearty laugh he asked,
"You gonna make it, bro?" The ladies giggled.
"Indeed I am!" I said as I shuffled past.

"Indeed?" he said in a mocking tone.
Turning to the ladies, he pointed at me with his umbrella.
"Listen to this guy! Indeed!"

I stumbled clumsily over nothing and froze.
He chuckled and the ladies giggled.

"Have you seen Muhammad Ali lately?"
I said with my back to them.
They fell silent.
"Yeah," he said with some apprehension.
"Well, me and Ali . . ." I barked, turning quickly,
with both fists cocked.
I lunged toward him.
He flinched.
"We have a little something in common!"

Startled, he smiled a less menacing smile.
I smiled, knowing he knew what I was talking about.

"Well, you have a good one, bro. Take care of yourself," he said, with eyes down, looking at the tip of his umbrella as he tapped it on the ground.

"You too," I said, looking back at the trio.
"And be good. I don't wanna have to come back here and kick your ass!"

He chuckled. "Indeed!"

WHAT HAPPENED TO YOUR HEAD?

I found the warmth of the sun on my hairless scalp healing.
Sitting alone at an outdoor café, sipping espresso,
I watched as he lumbered down the street;
his deliberate amble was amusing
with arms flapping loosely at his sides.

There was a focus in his eyes.
Looking around, I came to realize
that I was the object of his interest.

"Hello!" he bellowed as he approached.
He was not quite right.

"How are you?" I replied.
"What happened to your head?" he blurted.
"I had brain surgery."

He leaned in close to examine the fresh scars.

"Wow! Did it hurt?" he asked, continuing his examination.
"A little," I replied.
"Does it hurt now?" he asked.
"Nope."
"What's wrong with you?"

I smiled. His childlike curiosity was refreshing.

"I have Parkinson's disease," I replied.

He stepped back a bit, taking in the whole scene,
looking at me, at the café, at the other tables, and back to my head.
"Do you take pills?" he asked.
"Yes, I—"
"I take pills too. What's wrong with you again?"
"I have Parkinson's disease."
"Right. I've heard of that. I can't sleep and have lots of dreams."

I nodded and began to ask a question of my own,
but apparently our time together was up.

"Well, it looks like it hurts," he blurted. "Bye."

And with that he was gone.

I watched as he went on his way,
arms flapping loosely at his sides.
He was not a half a block down the street
when he stopped an unwitting couple
and pointed in my direction.
"He had brain surgery!" he exclaimed, loud enough for all to hear.
Smiling at the trio, I waved and pointed to the scars on my head.

I sat back and took another sip of my espresso,
and again noticed the warmth of the sun on my hairless scalp . . .

How refreshing!

HIS NUMBER

everyone at the tourist-trap street-side café
suddenly found their mediocre meals delightful
and their banal conversations fascinating

diverting their gaze with faux interest
in bad food and small talk as he approached
collecting money for the homeless

wild-eyed and with an edge of madness
he went about unwittingly, extending
the noble endeavors of ineffectual men to the streets

I looked him in the eye as he advanced
his menacing scowl turned to a maniacal grin
relishing his gift for creating unease

he barked a caustic *fuck you!* at the table next to mine
unwilling were they to engage in his little game of *give or else*
where homelessness is just a pretense for making us squirm

I looked him in the eye and smiled
how are you? I asked
pulling a couple of bucks from my pocket

you heard me, brother! he said as we shook hands
eyeing the other tables, *fuckers!*
easy now, I said with some force

I tightened my grip and pulled him close, *play nice*
surprised, he looked at me and winked
and I knew

that he knew

that I had his number

SUNDAY MORNING IN THE VILLAGE

fruit flies swarm cherries, eating dreams from a Dumpster
an opossum waddles through the silent city morning
scavenging scraps, dashing the hopes of a rat
in an alley where a drunk pisses a sigh of relief
and steel-caged stores turn the city
like an inside-out prison
into something more welcoming
to flies and rats than the five tourists
wandering down the bleak street
that buzzed with promise just hours ago
was it Chicago that never sleeps?

a traffic light silently cycles from red to green to yellow and back
signaling no one as the village slumbers behind drawn shades
hangovers and whores
addicts and actors
cabbies and clerks
street vendors and public works

amused, an old man on a park bench
heavy-faced and a bottle of rum
chuckles at the irony of the Hawaiian shirt

and the fruit flies keep at it

PRAGMATICS

The place was empty. Just me and her.
She appeared eager to spring into service as I approached.
She was way too chipper for 6 a.m.

I'll have a small coffee, cream, no sugar.

The words that followed made my head hurt.

Medium is the smallest we have.

The words careened through my noggin.
How can that be? Do the math!

The words hung in the silence.

Medium is the smallest we have.

I stood looking directly into her eyes.
I noticed the mole on her cheek and the wisp of hair on her forehead.
She stared back.
The silence got loud.

A palpable tension filled the room.

There we stood in a twisted standoff, as if waiting for Sergio Leone to yell, *Cut!*

The haunting whistle of a soundtrack by Ennio Morricone filled my head.

Tongue-tied we stood.

Waiting.

In silence.

It got awkward.

Just as it got unbearable, I noticed the sign above her head:

Medium. Large. And something called *The Great One.*

Right she was.

On second thought, make that a medium.

PART 6

THORNS

◆ ◆ ◆

There is nothing more dreadful than the habit of doubt. Doubt separates people. It is a poison that disintegrates friendships and breaks up pleasant relations. It is a thorn that irritates and hurts; it is a sword that kills.

—Buddha

◆ ◆ ◆

THE JOURNEY

the journey begins the same for all of us
wide-eyed and openmouthed
the experiences that shape us unfold

a vicious dog's bite
a father's drunken tirade
a loving mother's sudden death

from day one, wide eyes begin to narrow
open mouths draw tight
in fear of rejection, humiliation, or loss

through paper-clip eyes in a cardboard-cutout world
paralyzed, unable to
pet a dog, realize potential, or open up to love

history repeats the same defeats, time and again
in a cycle of fear of what you know
and what you do not

FEAR RIDES THE SUBWAY

the stench of a New York City subway
in a midsummer rush-hour crowd

sitting, standing, so close and so far
face-to-face, shoulder to shoulder
with eyes down, looking anywhere but here
pretending not to notice anyone or anything

fear listens but does not hear
the man babbling to no one about his mother
the addict moaning in the corner
the mother screaming at her kids

fear separates one from another
in this uneasy world, we steady ourselves
hand over hand, on the subway, together
rattling, station to station, through life

so near and so far
fear looks around
but does not see
that we
are all
one

VOWS

a dank, dark alley
a place more hospitable to roaches and rats
than the old man slouched against a Dumpster
swigging cheap wine from a screw-top jug

he tells himself he was a good man
and he did good things
confused by life's irony
alone on the streets he sits with his sins

and the bright lights of a hotel hall illuminate
the young and the old, the bitter and the oblivious
the angry and the disillusioned, as they drink
plastered-on smiles, teetering on high hopes

the bridesmaid downs another shot of tequila
her hair let down like all who desire
the best man takes a long tug on a bottle of beer
his tie undone, his yearning unanswered

they gather today to toast bride and groom
as they vow to preserve the blunders of their upbringing
embracing their parents' mistakes
as their own

when the bright lights dim
and the hall goes silent and dark
the sounds of the street begin to stir
anger in even the best of men

as he is staggering down a knife's edge
through loathsome streets
he trips over an old man in the alley
Goddamn good-for-nothing bum!

in a dank, dark alley
a place more hospitable to roaches and rats
the best man slouches against a Dumpster
swigging fine bourbon from a brown paper bag

he tells himself he is a good man
and he does good things
trying hard to forget
he sits with his sins

JUDGMENT

how many times have I passed you?

how many times have I glanced and turned away
afraid to look into your eyes?

how many times have I approached you
only to steer clear, uncertain, tentative?

how many times have you asked
only to watch as I, like so many others
divert my gaze to the sky, to the sidewalk
anywhere but your weathered face?

and how many times have you forced us all to look into the mirror
relishing your ability to hold sway
next to the bank machine
or at the restaurant window?

many times we've passed judgment
as we passed each other in the rain and in the snow
in the thick, hot air of August and frigid winds of January

many times I've wanted to stop
look into your steel-blue eyes
dulled by circumstance
and ask your story

how many times have you thought
the fucker's wearing one-hundred-dollar shoes and won't give me shit?

actually, I gave you five dollars last time I saw you
you said *thank you,* I said *no problem*
our eyes met for more than a moment
I saw the corners of your mouth turn up—a slight smile?

I'll give you something when next I see you
and I may just ask you your name

TO BE FREE

oh, to be free
free to choose
from countless brands of shampoo
triple-acting ultraclean with balsam
or extragentle megahold with protein
or hydrating or clarifying or volumizing
which isn't even a word

free to choose
from countless brands of toilet paper
unscented and quilted
or scented with ripples
or plain with aloe and vitamin E
free to pamper your ass

free to choose
from countless brands of cereal
frosted, puffed, or toasted
with honey-oat bunches
or multigrain banana bursts
or triple-berry fiber-bran honey-cluster cookie crisp
free to choose from so much new and improved original formula ultra
shit most of the world could not possibly fathom

oh, to be free
free to live in a home on six acres of land
with five bedrooms, four baths, and a three-car garage
for two people

free to complain about paying four bucks for a gallon of gas and
sixty bucks to fill the tank of a vehicle that gets ten miles per gallon and
free to bitch about how difficult it is getting in and out of the parking
lot at the coffee shop where you just spent five bucks for a double tall
vanilla soy latte, extra wet
whatever that is

free to
display a flag made in China
on your car made in Japan
because you're proud to be an American

oh, to be free
free to file a lawsuit against the manufacturer of the iron that seared
your chest as you got the wrinkles out of the shirt you were wearing
because they didn't explicitly tell you
that's a bad idea!

free to file a lawsuit against the company that served you the hot cup of
coffee that you proceeded to dump in your lap, scalding your balls
because they didn't explicitly tell you
coffee is hot, don't spill it on your balls!

free from responsibility, free from accountability
free not to have to suffer the consequences of being an idiot

free in a country with two million of its citizens in prison
more than any other country in the world

free in a country that spends $700 billion a year on defense
over a trillion dollars a year in total defense-related stuff
and free to hold a bake sale to raise money for armor for your son
that a trillion bucks did not cover

free to live in a country where
CEOs make seventy-eight times as much salary
five hundred times as much
in total compensation as an average worker
while fifty million live without health care
forty-six million live in poverty—including 16.4 million children
3.5 million homeless in a given year
nearly one million on any given day

freedom
some people are willing to die for it
some have no choice

THESE DAYS, MORE OFTEN THAN NOT...

I understand
on the train reading the paper on their way to work
at the market, with their kids picking through fresh corn
or walking around the lake hand in hand on a crisp fall day

they have all had dark days
some are in the middle of the pitch right now
as they try to make sense of today and wonder
with apprehension about tomorrow

I want to let them know it's going to be okay
things work out, always and without fail
still I have dark days of judgment

on the highway as if no one else exists
in the store as they tell their kids to *shut up*
in the coffee shop confidently expressing their individuality
in the only way they know how:
double tall soy latte, extra wet (I'm still not sure what that means)

but these days, more often than not, I understand
I want to let them know it's going to be okay
things work out, always and without fail

things are rarely what they seem and never are they what you expect
sometimes the brightest light is behind you
or it may be dim, so dim you walk away into darkness
but it is there, always and without fail

as I feel my body letting me down
I am struck by the light that picks me up
time and again, always and without fail
with fewer days of disdain in my heart

THE OCEAN IS MY TEACHER

it is 1 a.m. and I can't move
it is 1 a.m. and I can't think
it is 1 a.m. and I am at the helm
trying to navigate from here to there

through an ocean of uncertainty, doubt rears its head
with each wave that crashes over the bow
and each gust that howls through the rigging

it is dark and the seas are rough, making it difficult to distinguish
the poise and self-assurance of a brilliant night sky
from the self-doubt and apprehension of the deep that lies ahead

though I know stars shine bright
behind the clouds above
it is of little solace now

in the middle of night
in the middle of nowhere
in the middle of a struggle
to make my way home

It is 5 a.m. and I can't move
it is 5 a.m. and I can't think
it is 5 a.m. and I am at the helm
trying to navigate from here to there

the sun slowly reveals the horizon
shedding light and providing clarity
as trepidation gives way to certainty

the optimism of the morning after a night in the pitch
lifts me once again
from these angry waters

I know a storm is always brewing
a thick fog is always lurking
and the ocean is always teaching

in the middle of night
in the middle of nowhere
in the middle of a struggle
to make my way home

EASING INTO TRAFFIC

my body sinks into the seat
as I accelerate down the freeway
I turn on the radio and settle in for the ride . . .

when I'm cut off by too many bills to pay,
a broken window, and peeling white paint

cut off by testicular cancer, the heart attack,
child support, and the unemployment line

cut off by cat puke on the carpet, bad hair day,
the hangover, and keeping up with the Joneses

the anonymous, passing aggressive as they work it out
on concrete and rubber, in metal and glass

I think I'll stay right here, in this lane

the lane for those who made love last night
for those who are listening to Miles Davis
for those who are gonna enjoy a cold beer this evening
while preparing dinner for the family

for those who heard the birds this morning
while sitting in the early mist of a beautiful spring day
sipping hot black coffee from a wood-fired stone mug

I'll stay in this lane, unhurried, alive,
and grateful
at least for today

ONLY ONE EXCEPTION

there is something to be said for the comfort
of a pair of worn shoes, a tattered T-shirt, and faded jeans
consoling and calming, like the blanket you never wanted to give up
when you were three years old

but the day arrives when you have to part with these comforts
it's the temporary nature of things, most things

there is something to be said for that first day of spring
not the calendar day, but the day you first notice the sun
sitting high in the sky as it warms you to the bone
reassuring after a long winter

there is something to be said for sticky summer days
that remind you of everything good in your youth
like a day at the beach, getting tossed about in the surf
digging your feet deep into the cool sand

and the contentment later that evening
as you settle in for a good sleep
the slight glow of sunburn soothed by the salt breeze
caressing your face as you nod off

there is something to be said for the melancholy of fall's vibrant colors
and the memory of a walk across campus
hand in hand with your love, jumping into piles of newly fallen leaves

like children experiencing everything for the very first time

and there is something to be said for being snowed in
on a frigid Sunday afternoon in winter
sitting by the fire with your love watching the flames flicker
sipping port and not saying much, just being and loving

these days all come and go with each tick of time
it's the temporary nature of things, most things

like a great novel that leaves you wanting more
or an inspiring piece of music that moves you
to listen over and over because it keeps ending
they all end, eventually

I am forever clad in worn shoes, a tattered T-shirt, and faded jeans
as I stroll from the warmth of an endless spring day
to the perpetual summer of salt air and
a romp in an unending pile of autumn's leaves
to the eternal crackle of a fire in winter
engrossed in page after page of the greatest novel ever written
and awash in the exquisite sounds of the most beautiful symphony ever heard

I can think of only one exception
to the temporary nature of things
and that is
my love
for you

ALMOST NIRVANA

the people look like roses now
and the street is singing *A Love Supreme*

the putrid city has lost its edge

empty are the prisons
empty are the shelters
and the asylum walls ring silent

cobwebs cover gavels and pews
in empty courtrooms
in empty churches

no need for the evening news
no need for pundits and pulpits
no need for politicians and prophets

just Coltrane and roses now
beautiful roses . . .

the thorns!
you forgot the thorns!

MISFORTUNE AND HEARTACHE

I'd rather the sting of
misfortune and heartache
I'd rather the hurt of
hard luck and a bad break

I'd rather the anguish
as I strain to recall
your smile, your eyes
than nothing at all

PART 7

BLOSSOMS

◆ ◆ ◆

When you realize how perfect everything is you will tilt your head back and laugh at the sky.

—Buddha

◆ ◆ ◆

SAILING WITH STRAVINSKY

the howl of wind sliced through the rigging
driving rain like bird shot into my face
and I thought, *can a bassoon really anger?*

the ocean staged a savage ballet of whitecaps high above my head
a violent, unpredictable dance beneath me
and I thought, *how is it possible that music and dance can infuriate so?*

another wall of ocean crashes into the cockpit
knocking me to the deck
this is life! I thought as I struggled to my feet
the fury of twenty-foot waves and sixty-knot winds

and I thought of the passion, the emotion
of grown men coming to blows in the aisles
in the riot that ensued that evening in 1913
when Stravinsky unleashed *The Rite of Spring*

no fanciful footwork
no amorous stuff of fluffy ballet dreams
ugly pagans sacrificed a maiden to satisfy the gods of spring

as nature unleashes its fury upon me
in the middle of the ocean
I thought, *I wonder if Stravinsky was a sailor?*

ME AND WALTER AND MY '74 HORNET

"I said blues in F. What the fuck are you playing?"

I don't recall his name. He was studious looking and pompous sounding. And he was not playing the blues in F.

"Well, Mr. Bishop, the way I see it . . ."

This ought to be good, I thought. I was eager to hear the rest of whatever he had to say, but never got the chance. Walter cut him off midsentence.

"The way I see it is the blues is something you should know. Now get the fuck away from my piano."

And with that class ended.

"Anyone got a car?" Walter asked.
"Yeah, I do," I said. He had to catch a bus back to New York City.

Now, here is a guy who ought to have a limo shuttling him around, not some white Miles-wannabe from the burbs with a beat-up '74 Hornet. I mean, this is Walter Bishop Jr. we're talking about! He's gigged with Bird, Miles, Sonny, and Blakey, just to name a few!

"Cool car," he said, looking around at the sparse dash and three on the column as he settled into the passenger's seat, with legs so long his knees nearly touched the dash.

"Thanks," I replied.

"You smoke?" he asked.

"No," I said.

"Mind if I do?"

"Not at all," I replied.

Walter sparked a joint.
"Oh, *that* smoke," I said. "Sure."

And that was the first joint I would smoke with Walter Bishop Jr. on our many rides to the bus station in my '74 Hornet.

Cool.
Very cool.

MILES DAVIS KNOCKS BUILDINGS OVER

Miles Davis knocks buildings over
tearing the roof off with one note
a single splat, like an uppercut
it swings so hard dropping you to the mat

Miles Davis knocks buildings over
kicking in the door with a tear
a nasty rip, like a right hook
it swings so hard reminding you who's hip

Miles Davis knocks buildings over
running the voodoo down, in a silent way
walkin' kind of blue, Miles smiles
from birth of the cool to bitches brew

never the old man with a cane
a legend now and still doing it
in his music and in his style
"how do ya like my shoes?"

knocking buildings over with silence

making you find your own way home
play it now; he'll tell you what it is later
if Miles were here, he'd tell you the same
in a one-word poem
Miles

RED SAILING CAP

I notice a fly on the bill of the red sailing cap perched upon my head as I sit by the fire watching the flames dance about in the breeze that gently blows through the yard behind our house on the hillside of a winding road in a small town with a lake just miles from the capital of a state that was one of the first in a country bordered by two great oceans that make up over half of this planet, the third from a sun and one of billions in a universe so vast that . . .

. . . I have to believe there is a red sailing cap on the head of another watching the flames of a fire dance about in the breeze . . . and I laughed

. . . when the fly buzzed on I wondered where it would land next . . . and I laughed.

"Andy! Did you hear anything I just said?"

FOR YOU, I WOULD HAVE DONE ANYTHING

In memory of Sinbad

I remember the bowl of chips on the table
they were your favorite
I knew that when I bought them

I remember the satisfied look on your face
as you delicately pulled a chip from the bowl
between thumb and index finger

with pinky extended
you carefully placed it in your mouth
a ceremony reserved for oysters and caviar

I remember the crunch and the audible hum of satisfaction
"Mmm, my favorite!" you said with eyes closed
"I got them for you," I said

I was struck by the sincerity and the look in your eyes
when, after some internal deliberation, you replied
"You did that for me?"

I would have done anything for you
but this, this bowl of chips, was to be my last chance to do anything
for you

a bowl of chips, for Christ's sake!

I remember that bowl of chips as I walk through the door
and see Tyler and Josa at the kitchen table

I'm thinking of Tyler
sorry he will never hear your laugh
as we exchange stories of our long past together

I'm thinking of your parents
sitting down to dinner now
eating in silence, together and alone

I'm thinking of your wife sitting on the deck
as the sun sets over the city
sipping a glass of wine, silent and alone

and I am thinking of you on that last day I saw you
you knew then, didn't you
you knew how, where, and when, and . . .
I remember that bowl of chips
a bowl of chips, for Christ's sake
the last opportunity I would have
to do something
anything
for you

CROW

the insufferable cackle of a crow
makes me chuckle

my eyes pop open
I pull myself up off the bed
a sleepy *good morning* whispers behind me

I turn to see her smile—a smile I remember waking up to every morning
a smile that disappeared some time back
it is nice to see that smile again

good morning, babe, I say
as I pull the door open
and step into another day

what's so funny, crow?
why are you cackling so?
what do you know that I do not?

the cackle of an insufferable crow
makes me wonder

BLOSSOM

the safety of distance
wrapped tight in a delicate bud
is more painful
than just letting it
blossom

THIS THOUGHT

even the most delicate thought
can go on forever

nothing is as authentic
nothing is as beautiful
as this notion

in this transient life
it is only the intangible
ideas, concepts, beliefs
that last

people die
buildings rot
empires collapse
we all cease to be

but this delicate thought
can go on
forever

SOMETIMES

sometimes
with the sunlight in my eyes
I am blind to the road

sometimes
words are not there
I search to no avail

nothing, empty
I keep at it
like the dull ache of a sore tooth
I can't stop poking

and sometimes
a flower guides me
with the sunlight in my eyes
I can see the road
plain as day

TITLE OF THIS POEM

this line is the first line of another poem
and this is the second

that is about all I know about
writing poetry
and really all I need

enough to get it out
so I don't keep it in

enough to make light of it
so I don't get too heavy

enough to keep me up
so I don't get down

just enough

this is the second-to-last line
and this, the last

AFTERWORD

This collection of poems was inspired by my desire to understand Parkinson's disease (PD), with which I was diagnosed in 2001. I began writing these words the day I was finally diagnosed and have not stopped. It was never my intention to share them with anyone other than my family and a few close friends. It was never my intention to become a *poet*—I just had to write, and this is what came out. This was simply creative therapy, my way of coping with the illness.

When I read the first few poems to my wife, Josa, it became apparent that these words were important for her. They provided a degree of understanding and insight into my days. And as I shared them with others, I discovered that I could have my therapy and perhaps help people in a similar position. Living with disease is not a solo trip; it is a family affair. Josa has benefited from these words in her own struggle with PD. It is my hope that these words speak to others who suffer from PD and to their loved ones. It is my hope that these words speak to anyone living with illness, loss, or isolation.

◆ ◆ ◆

I say *finally* diagnosed because it took some time to zero in on the disease. Parkinson's disease is not something you wake up with one day and say, "I have Parkinson's disease." It comes on slowly over the course of a year or two. It dawdles along, snatching a cell here and a cell there, leisurely seizing one's ability to move, leaving a personification of itself in its plodding wake.

Additionally, PD is not easily diagnosed. Although there are no lab tests to definitively diagnose Parkinson's disease, patients will often undergo a series of tests—blood tests, urine tests, CT scans, MRI scans—to exclude the possibility of other disorders. Ultimately, diagnosis requires a systematic neurological exam by a movement disorder specialist. The exam includes testing reflexes and muscle strength throughout the body, coordination, balance, and other details of movement.

The original title of this collection was *Substantia Nigra*. (I was advised that perhaps that title was a bit obscure, so *Renegade Pinky* it is.) Substantia nigra, literally meaning "black substance," refers to a small region in the brain stem, just above the spinal cord. It is one of the centers that help control movement. Cells within the substantia nigra produce dopamine, a neurotransmitter responsible for transmitting signals from one nerve cell to another within the brain. Among other things, dopamine produced in the substantia nigra helps control movement and balance, and is essential to the proper functioning of the central nervous system. Loss of dopamine causes critical nerve cells in the brain to fire out of control, leaving people unable to direct or control their movement in a normal manner.

Parkinson's disease is the direct result of the loss of dopamine-producing cells in the substantia nigra. The symptoms of PD emerge when the disease is well under way—when a person is down to the last 20 percent of dopamine-producing cells. I am struck by how forgiving the body is!

Primary symptoms of PD include tremor, rigidity of the limbs and trunk, slowness or loss of movement, and postural instability.

There are a myriad of other symptoms as well, including cluttered speech; impaired ability to swallow; drooling; difficulty interpreting social cues; impaired impulse control; difficulty prioritizing; insomnia; disturbingly vivid dreams; acting-out of dream content; hallucinations; loss of sense of smell; impaired spatial reasoning; dizziness and fainting; weight loss; pain of the muscles, joints, and tendons attributable to tension; dystonia; rigidity; and injuries associated with attempts at accommodation.

❖ ❖ ❖

It was a Friday when I was diagnosed. Afterward, Josa and I went for lunch. We sat, silent. I looked across the table at her. She smiled and said, "We'll be fine."

I believed her.

"You can handle this, I know you can."

I believed her.

I took a sip of my beer and said the words aloud. "Parkinson's disease." I heard the words as if for the first time. "Parkinson's disease." Interesting. Who would have thought? So now what?

That night I did not sleep much. It was a long, dark, and lonely night. It was agonizing. My mind frantically raced from thought to thought. A thousand questions and concerns swirled through my head as I pondered the meaning of my diagnosis.

I finally fell into a deep sleep shortly before sunrise. My eyes popped open at about 7:30 a.m. Although my sleep was short, it was deep—one of those sleeps that leave you wondering who and where you are when you wake. Slowly I pulled myself from the fog, trying to recount the events of the day before. I remembered tamales and beer at lunch, and I remembered Josa saying, "You can handle this."

Handle this? Handle what?

I remembered the doctor's office. But why? What was it?

Then it hit me. Oh, yeah, I have a chronic degenerative disorder of the central nervous system for which there is no cure! Yikes!

I had to laugh, and laugh I did. Life comes at you sometimes, and sometimes you just gotta sit back and say, *Okay, I give!* We had just gone through a very costly medical situation that rendered us nearly penniless (a story for another time). Additionally, we were dealing with my ill father who was in need of twenty-four-hour care. I, with power of attorney, was having to manage his affairs and deal with family, doctors, attorneys, real estate agents, insurance agents, Title 19, and so on. On top of that I had just started a new business, we had just bought a new home, and we were in the process of adopting a child. Now this. *Okay, I give!*

Like a mindfulness bell it woke me. I felt alive. A sense of clarity and levity came over me. I felt oddly prepared to get on with this next phase of my life. I saw a fork in the road, and I saw it clearly: two paths and just one answer. Everything in my life has prepared me for this moment. I don't judge my luck. I accept it for what it is, a simple fact and out of my control. My journey is set. Each step along the way is the only step. No looking back. No looking forward. There is only this step. And so it goes. I have Parkinson's disease. This must be a gift!

~Andy

ACKNOWLEDGMENTS

The poems in this humble collection were encouraged and inspired by many, and I most want to thank my wife and dearest friend, Josa. Her undying love has been my salvation, and her words on that Friday at a Mexican restaurant in Hartford several years ago ring through my head when the going gets rough: "You can do this." She has provided support and encouragement whenever called upon and has suffered through countless readings at all times of the day and night. And to our son, Tyler, who reminds us daily that unconditional love is unconditional and that superheroes really do exist.

These words owe much to my mother, Jackie Ganem, for her love and understanding during these tumultuous times and throughout my life. And to my sisters, Annie and Sarah Weatherwax, whose own creativity and support the past several years have given me inspiration to keep going. I would also like to thank JoAnn Cavallaro, Joyce Kauffman, and Eileen Graham; you are all great friends, and I am blessed to have you in my life. And special thanks to Annie and Joyce for putting us up, and putting up with us, on our frequent trips to Mass General.

And to my father, Bill, who passed away just three months after the arrival of Tyler, I say thank you. I am who I am because you were who you were.

I extend my deepest appreciation to my business partners Bill Hunt and Jeremy Sanchez, whose patience and understanding these past years mean so much to me. I could not ask for better partners and friends. And to the entire GSI team for your dedication and hard work; thanks for picking up any slack that I may have placed on your desk. You guys rock! Thank you all so much.

This book has benefited from the encouragement and editorial input of my good friend Michael Burgan (a.k.a. Yeti), whose friendship since that fateful walkathon in sixth grade means so much to me. Additionally, I am grateful for the editorial input of Tom and Isabelle Smith, and the enthusiasm of my nephew and kindred spirit Nick Saint Onge.

Special thanks to the Meeting House Poets, who've helped me realize I may just be a poet after all! (There. I said it. I'm a poet. I feel better now!)

I would also like to acknowledge Chela and George Saint Onge; their children Graciela, Nicholas, and Peter; Alex Misch and her children Charlie, Zachary, and Michael; and Andrew Smith, son of Isabelle and Tom. Where would we be without family?

And to the outstanding staff at the Massachusetts General Hospital Movement Disorders Unit, especially my neurologist Alice Flaherty, I could not have done all I did these past several years without your help. And to DBS programmer and nurse practitioner Lisa Townsend, and neurosurgeon Emad "it goes to eleven" Eskandar, I say thank you. The work you do is nothing short of amazing.

I extend my deepest gratitude to the sangha at Buddhist Faith Fellowship, especially Glen, for your dedication and hard work; to Brian, Ron, and Stephen, for your support and good humor; and to Kate and Sue, you are in my prayers. *Metta*. I would also like to thank Mark Unno and the broader sangha at Barre Center for Buddhist Studies. *Gassho*.

Special thanks go to Reverend Richard Allen; you are a source of great inspiration! And the entire congregation of South Church, especially my dear friends Paul and Jane DeMaio. You've all contributed to my understanding of hope. You've all contributed to my understanding of what it means to live in the present moment, wisely and earnestly. You've all contributed to my understanding that peace is here and now and that the miracle is not walking on water—the miracle is walking on earth!

Many thanks to my friends at the Connecticut Parkinson's Working Group; I always feel like I've arrived home on those Saturday mornings. I wish you all the very best.

Special thanks to Ken Dubrowski for the terrific chapter illustrations. Thank you, Ken, for your perseverance and generosity. And more thanks to my sister Annie for the wonderful cover art. You are the source of great inspiration!

And to all the people I've met on my journey, including Mary, who is living with PD, and her husband, Frank, who has to live with and care for Mary. Thank you for not running away as I approached you on the streets of New York City with shaved head and scars still fresh. Thank you for accepting my poems and for reading them. And thank you both for that phone call Christmas Day 2007 that made me realize the power of words. I am glad I could help. And Jimmy, who was homeless and now is not, I am glad I mustered the courage to ask you your story, and I am grateful you mustered the courage to share it with me. And Kim, who told me about losing her mother, father, and brother to cancer last year as we sat on a broken-down Metro North train in the sweltering heat of August for three hours. Hang in there, Kim; your suffering is a gift. And to all the others I've met along the way, I wish you all the best.

Lastly, I would like to extend my deepest appreciation to my late mother-in-law (that's right, my mother-in-law!), Graziella Smith, whose creative journey and spiritual mentorship have been an inspiration. Remember, G, embrace the dysfunction! And to Peter Saint Onge, whose tender soul and creative spirit lives on in all of us who were so fortunate to have known him. In life he was an inspiration. In death he is my teacher. Thank you, Peter.

ABOUT THE MICHAEL J. FOX FOUNDATION

For the Michael J. Fox Foundation for Parkinson's Research, there is one clear measure of success: delivering better treatments and, ultimately, a cure to people living with Parkinson's disease. The foundation takes a focused and proactive approach to speeding scientific solutions that will improve patients' quality of life and works to maximize impact by pushing basic discoveries toward clinical trials and strategically targeting resources toward critical research hurdles. Now the largest private funder of Parkinson's research worldwide, the foundation has invested more than $297 million in research since founded in 2000.

TEAMFOX Team Fox is the grassroots fundraising program of the Michael J. Fox Foundation. Launched in January 2006, Team Fox is made up of thousands of people across the globe who find fun and creative ways to raise funds and awareness for the foundation and Parkinson's research. Since the program's inception, this diverse community of change-makers has raised nearly $20 million for Parkinson's research and continues to grow and exceed expectations. Join Team Fox today at www.teamfox.com.

All proceeds from the sale of this book go to the Michael J. Fox Foundation for Parkinson's Research.

COVER ART AND CHAPTER ILLUSTRATIONS

The cover art is from a painting by my talented sister, artist and writer Annie Weatherwax. The painting is based on a photo she took of me the day after deep brain stimulation (DBS) surgery. And, my good friend, illustrator, woodworker, and all-around great guy Ken Dubrowski is responsible for the chapter illustrations.

CHAPTER QUOTATIONS

Michael J. Fox, *ThinkExist*,
   http://en.thinkexist.com/quotes/michael_j._fox/

Muhammad Ali, *ThinkExist*,
   http://en.thinkexist.com/quotes/Muhammad_Ali/

Buddha, *ThinkExist*,
   http://en.thinkexist.com/quotes/Buddha/

Jimmy Dean, *ThinkExist*,
   http://en.thinkexist.com/quotes/Jimmy_Dean/

Epicurus, *ThinkExist*,
   http://en.thinkexist.com/quotes/Epicurus/

CPSIA information can be obtained at www.ICGtesting.com
Printed in the USA
BVOW031332041212

307266BV00001B/6/P